Tidewater Virginia
A Picture Book to Remember Her By

CRESCENT BOOKS
NEW YORK

CLB 1975
© 1988 Colour Library Books Ltd., Guildford, Surrey, England.
Printed and bound in Barcelona, Spain by Cronion, S.A.
All rights reserved.
1988 edition published by Crescent Books, distributed by Crown Publishers, Inc.
ISBN 0 517 64413 4
h g f e d c b a

Thomas Jefferson once wrote: "Our country being much intersected with waters and trade brought generally to our doors, instead of being obliged to go in quest of it, has probably been one of the causes why we have no towns of any consequence." Jefferson, himself a product of Tidewater Virginia, underestimated the legacy it would leave us. The names on the land east of Richmond are among the most historic anywhere in America; names such as Yorktown and Williamsburg, Jamestown and Hampton Roads. But it is people who make a land, and no place in the history of America has produced more men and women who have made such a difference. The list includes such names as Carter and Byrd, Randolph and Mason, not to mention Thomas Jefferson, Patrick Henry and George Washington.

It was the site of the first permanent English settlement in North America, established at Jamestown more than a dozen years before the Pilgrims set foot on Plymouth Rock up in Massachusetts, explaining with pious innocence that they thought Tidewater Virginia extended that far north.

It doesn't. It extends inland as far as the Fall Line, which was for generations the western boundary of England's colonies in America, and north to the mouth of the Potomac. From the north and the south, a network of rivers and streams come together to empty into the James, York and Rappahannock Rivers, all of which were perfect highways for the original settlers to penetrate the thick forest that covered the Tidewater back in 1607, when Captain Christopher Newport and a company of men who called themselves Venturers arrived in the Chesapeake Bay with instructions to establish a colony on a river that bent to the northwest. The people in London who came up with the idea had nothing more in mind than that a river flowing northwest was the most likely to lead to the fabulous Orient on the other side. They didn't know that all the rivers in the Tidewater are inclined in that direction. Nor did they know that none of them led to the Pacific. Captain Newport did as he was told and sailed up the first river he came to, the James. He sailed a fair distance inland until he found a peninsula that seemed protected from possible attack by sea or by land.

They were attacked many times, by Indians and disease over land, and by other hungry settlers from over the sea. They found the climate all but intolerable, and when they weren't fighting outsiders they fought among themselves. But somehow, though the odds were against them, they managed to survive and to thrive.

They were not the first white settlers in the Tidewater. Sir Walter Raleigh's colony on Roanoke Island, further south in what is now North Carolina, had vanished without trace, but not before Raleigh had gone back to London full of enthusiasm for tobacco. The English liked the stuff, but in the absence of a source in North America they had developed a preference for tobacco grown in Spain. The new Virginians dedicated themselves to refining a strain that could be fashionable in London. By the mid-1600s they had found the right formula and business became so good they had to send to England for more people to help them clear the forest and grow more of the weed.

Most of those who came considered England to be their real home. But their children had other ideas. By the 18th century the Tidewater was populated by Englishmen who had never crossed the ocean. America was their home, and the sons of the Tidewater had more to do with shaping the events and ideas that would become the American tradition than any group of men in any of the former English colonies.

The tradition is kept alive in the Tidewater in the form of magnificent Colonial plantations, in the restoration of Virginia's old capital at Williamsburg and in historic sites that are at every turn in the road. But even without its proud history, Tidewater Virginia would be well-known as one of the most beautiful places on the Eastern Seaboard of the United States. The rivers still curve to the northwest, but nobody cares that they don't lead to the riches of Cathay. There are riches enough right there to satisfy anybody who enjoys watching the sun rise over the water or catching a glimpse of a deer hiding in the tall grass. Who could resist listening to the birds in an azalea-filled plantation garden or walking along a dusty road hidden under the high arches of carefully-spaced elm trees? The Tidewater is a place apart, with a strong pull to quieter times when life was far from easy, but the pace was liveable.

Facing page: sunset silhouettes the statue of Captain John Smith at Jamestown.

Virginia Beach (above and top left) is famous for its marvelous surf and long, warm summers. In recent years it has acquired a reputation as one of Virginia's smartest holiday centers. As might be expected at such an attractive resort, private frontage (top) on the beach is at a premium. Throughout the Chesapeake Bay area there are beaches renowned for their fine sands (left) and unspoilt beauty.

The granite cross (above) at Cape Henry is a memorial to the first English settlers to arrive on the shores of the New World. After a difficult winter voyage that lasted over three months, the crew sighted land in April, 1607. Prior to journeying up the James River, they erected a high wooden cross at the place where they landed on Cape Henry, to claim the land for God and King James I of England. Today's cross was presented by the National Society of Daughters of the American Colonists in 1935 and marks the spot where the old cross stood. It is known as the First Landing Cross and is a National Historic Landmark.

Also at Cape Henry stands the Cape Henry Light (right). This striking black and white structure is the tallest cast-iron lighthouse in the United States and has a far-ranging, 160,000 candlepower electric light. It was built in 1881 to guide merchant shipping through the difficult passages of Chesapeake Bay. The shifting sand banks, bewildering tides and shallow water of the channels have always demanded skill of a ship's navigator. Indeed, the first colonists nearly came to grief whilst attempting to land at Cape Henry. Conscientiously maintained by the Coast Guard, the lighthouse is still in use today.

The shores of Virginia (these pages) have been popular with vacationers for generations and a thriving tourist industry has grown up to serve the visitors. One of the sights of Virginia Beach is the Chesapeake Bay Bridge-Tunnel (above), which stretches seventeen miles to connect Virginia Beach with the state's eastern shore and is one of the engineering wonders of the world.

The Portsmouth Lightship (above), on the Elizabeth River in downtown Portsmouth, is now a museum after serving for 48 years at sea. The museum contains a wealth of exhibits about the Coast Guard and the Lightship Service. Top: the marina on Lake Rudee and (inset) the mysterious swamplands that are part of the Seashore State Park on Cape Henry. Right: one of the many displays illustrating the history of flight at the Visitor Center of N.A.S.A.'s Langley Research Center near Hampton, Virginia.

Situated on Chesapeake Bay, the city of Norfolk is also graced by the Elizabeth River, and the riverfront (above and left) is one of its main leisure areas. Norfolk has a history as a naval base, and as such was prominent in the Second World War. Today, a variety of aircraft-carriers and battleships from the United States' Atlantic fleet may be observed at the dockyards (overleaf) beside ocean-going liners and merchant ships. Fine angling is assured all along the coastline of the Bay as fish thrive in these waters, and piers are provided for the harvest of the riches (facing page). A number of angling competitions are held throughout the season and prove to be very well-supported. It is hard not to catch fish in Chesapeake Bay!

13

The history of Norfolk (these pages) has always been connected with its position as an ideal seaport. It has deep water, plenty of anchorages and is well-protected from storms. From its founding in 1682, it has been a significant trading port, which led to its strategic importance during both the War of Independence and the Civil War. Indeed, it was burned down just before the former by the British and a cannonball is still lodged in the walls of one of the city's churches. Today, Norfolk is the headquarters of the United States' Atlantic fleet.

April is one of the most colorful months in Norfolk Botanical Gardens (these pages) because it is then that the azaleas bloom. Visitors to the gardens find them full of flowers that form a magnificent backdrop for the various statues, lakes and fountains to be found in the grounds.

When Fort Monroe, near Hampton, was built between 1819 and 1823 it was America's largest stone fort, and now contains showpieces such as the Casement Museum, home of the U.S. Army's Coast Artillery Museum (above), the Centurion Chapel (top), a howitzer (inset top) and the Lincoln Gun (inset bottom). Right: a cannon at Yorktown.

THE LINCOLN GUN

CAST IN 1860, THIS WAS THE
FIRST 15-INCH RODMAN GUN. ITS
RANGE WAS MORE THAN FOUR
MILES. WEIGHT OF THE PROJECTILE
WAS OVER 300 LBS. DURING CIVIL
WAR IT WAS USED TO BOMBARD
CONFEDERATE BATTERIES ON
SEWELLS POINT. THE GUN WAS
NAMED FOR PRESIDENT LINCOLN
IN MARCH 1862.

1969

The War of Independence ended a[t] Yorktown in 1781 and battlefield cannon remain there today (far le[ft] and below) to mark the time whe[n] America became a nation in her own right. On October 18th the British surrender terms were agreed at Moore House (bottom an[d] facing page bottom), Yorktown, and 100 years later the Victory Monument (left) was erected ther[e] in memory of the event.

East of Williamsburg lies The Old Country (these pages), a family theme park at Busch Gardens. The Old Country is divided into seven European-style hamlets designed to give the visitor a taste of the countries of Europe as they once were.

The James River was the main highway for the Virginian colonists of the seventeenth and eighteenth centuries and they built their splendid plantation houses, such as Berkeley Plantation Mansion (bottom) and the imposing mansion of Carter's Grove (bottom right), within sight of its banks. The houses that remain today have much to offer those interested in Virginian history. The Carter's Grove residence, for example, was host to the patriots and presidents from Virginia's "First Families " for almost two centuries. Also near the river in Surry County, the Shirley Plantation Mansion (right) is still occupied by the descendants of the original owners, the Hill Carters and, like the Chippokes Plantation on which the Mansion House (below) stands, remains a working farm. Rolfe Warren House (bottom center) is also situated in Surry County.

The interior of the Georgian-style mansion of Carter's Grove (these pages) is a delight. The elegance of the decorative designs and the subtle profusion of fine craftsmanship to be found in the airy rooms are easy on the eye. The land upon which it is built was given by Robert "King" Carter to his daughter, Elizabeth, with the wish that it always be known as "Carter's Grove." Unfortunately, Carter Burwell, who built the mansion, died in 1755 within six months of its completion, but his achievement was gratefully remembered by his descendants as five generations of the family have since inherited his house. The mansion contains many antique pieces of furniture from the past three centuries, but is famous above all for its rooms of carved panelling in golden loblolly pine (top).

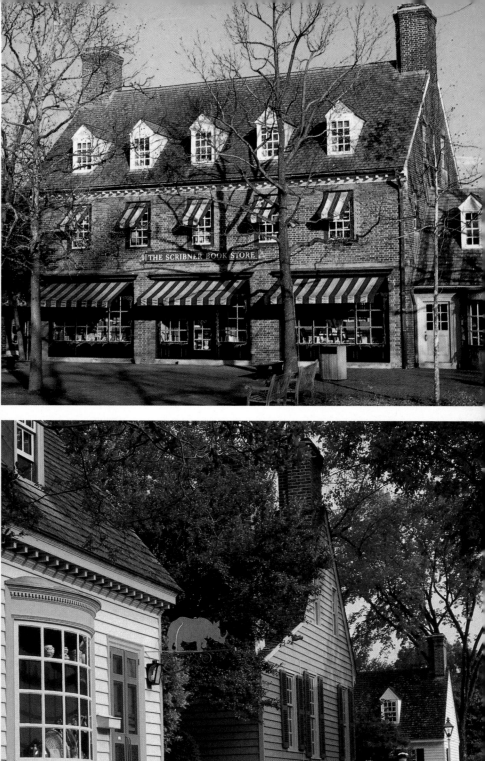

Colonial Williamsburg (these pages and overleaf) is rich in restored and reconstructed 18th-century buildings. The Governor's Palace (left), the Scribner Book Store (top), a Colonial Street house (above) and the Powder Magazine (overleaf) are among 45 buildings open to the public.

To heighten the feeling of history "coming alive" in Colonial Williamsburg, the visitor will see staff in 18th-century costume (these pages) performing colonial-style tasks as if time had stood still for two hundred years. So complete is the illusion that visitors appear to be trespassing on the past.

Military displays are staged throughout the year in Colonial Williamsburg (these pages). Participants wear authentic 18th-century dress and the weapons of the time are used throughout. The displays take place in Market Square, where cannon (bottom left) remain all year. Overleaf: the Timson House, Colonial Williamsburg.

The tangle of twentieth-century technology that is Busch Gardens' Loch Ness Monster Rollercoaster (left) contrasts starkly with the calm, eighteenth-century scenes recreated by the simple architecture of Duke of Gloucester Street (above) and the crisp, white lines of the Orlando Jones House, both in Colonial Williamsburg.

The statue of Pocahontas (top) in Jamestown honors the Indian chief's daughter who married an early settler, John Rolfe, in 1614 – a union that contributed to peace between the colonists and her tribe. Near Charles City stand two fine plantation mansions, Belle Air (above), the oldest frame house in America and a National Landmark, and Sherwood Forest Mansion (right), the home of President John Tyler. The latter dates from 1730 and is still owned by the Tyler family. Intriguingly, one particular room in the house is reputed to have been haunted for the past two hundred years by a ghost known as the Gray Lady. She is said to descend a staircase and sit in the Gray Room.

Sherwood Forest Mansion (these pages) still contains many of its original furnishings and color schemes. The authentic atmosphere thus created helps one to imagine the house in its heyday, with perhaps a curled and crinolined lady in residence. Indeed, these rooms, so perfect in their decoration, seem to be waiting for their former mistress to enter.

Jamestown, America's first English colony, contains a reconstruction of James Fort (these pages), from which the town grew, and features replicas of both the original cannon (bottom) and the first homes (right). Nearby are the foundations of the original buildings (below).

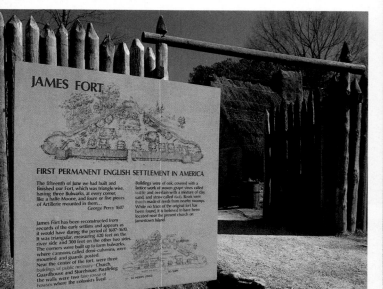

JAMES FORT

FIRST PERMANENT ENGLISH SETTLEMENT IN AMERICA

The fifteenth of June we had built and finished our Fort, which was triangle wise, having three Bulwarks, at every corner, like a halfe Moone, and foure or five pieces of Artillerie mounted in them...
George Percy 1607

James Fort has been reconstructed from records of the early settlers and appears as it would have during the period of 1607-1610. It was triangular, measuring 420 feet on the river side and 300 feet on the other two sides. The corners were built up to form bulwarks, where cannons called demi-culverins, were mounted and guards posted. Near the center of the fort, were three buildings of public necessity—Church, Guardhouse and Storehouse. Paralleling the walls were two faire rowse of howses where the colonists lived...

Buildings were of oak, covered with a lattice work of woven grape vines called wattle and overlain with a mixture of clay, sand, and straw called daub. Roofs were thatch made of reeds from nearby swamps. While no trace of the original fort has been found, it is believed to have been located near the present church on Jamestown Island.

Jamestown Festival Park (these pages) harbors replicas of the first ships sailed by the settlers into Chesapeake Bay: the *Susan Constant* (below), *Godspeed* and *Discovery*. Huts built to seventeenth-century design and costumed staff performing colonists' tasks complete the picture of Colonial Jamestown for the visitor.

49

Stratford Hall (these pages) is the home of the Lee family, whose most famous son, Robert E. Lee, is still honored in the South. Above: the nursery, with its miniature four-poster bed for the baby and tiny table and chairs, (top right) the kitchen, (far right) the blue bedroom, and (right) the parlor.

Popes Creek Plantation (top, above and facing page top near Wakefield, is the site of George Washington's birthplace and Stratford Hall (facing page bottom) is t birthplace of Robert E. Lee. Left: Oyster Creek.

George Washington was born on his father's Popes Creek Plantation (these pages) in February 1732. The house was destroyed during the War of Independence, and the buildings to be found there today are reconstructions. However, they are as close as possible in style and detail to the originals and the plantation is run today as a working farm according to the methods of Washington's time. On the site, the outline of the first president's birthplace is picked out in oyster shells above its safely-buried foundations.

One of the most famous houses in the country, Mount Vernon (these pages) was George Washington's home for almost fifty years. During that time he enlarged the house and added the various outbuildings. Left, far left and bottom: the Mansion, (below) the office and (below left) the interior of the Green House.

Alexandria stands across the Potomac River from Washington, D.C. and was founded in the 1730s by a group of Scottish merchants led by John Alexander, after whom the city is named. In its early history, the town was one of the most important in the country, especially as a tobacco distribution center. Fortunately, it was little damaged during the Civil War, and many of its oldest buildings have been preserved. The historic district of the city is designated a National Historic Landmark and contains nearly 100 blocks in the center of the original town, many of which exhibit examples of colonial and Federal architecture. Right, below and facing page top: an inviting mixture of shops on Washington Street, and (below right) St. Asaph Street blossoms. Characteristic of many Alexandria houses are shutters and clapboarding, as seen in Columbus Street (facing page bottom left) and also in King Street (facing page bottom right).

One of Alexandria's finest buildings is the George Washington Masonic National Memorial (right and top), built by Freemasons to honor the president who was one of their early members. The Lyceum (above) in Alexandria was built in the last century and today houses artifacts from the War of Independence. Inset top: Alexandria's Lloyd House, a fine example of Georgian architecture, and (inset bottom) the brightly-painted brickwork of Washington Street, Alexandria.

Top insets: spectators watch the changing of the guard at the Tomb of the Unknowns (overleaf) in Arlington National Cemetery (inset far left and above). The Memorial Amphitheatre (left) is used for Veteran Day services at the cemetery, which contains the graves of John F. Kennedy (inset bottom right) and his brother, Robert (inset bottom left). Top: the U.S. Marine Corps War Memorial at Arlington. As the flag flies it lends life to this magnificent bronze.